LET'S
see

The
Washington Monument

by Marc Tyler Nobleman

Content Adviser: Linda B. Lyons, Independent Historian and Education Chair,
Art Deco Society of Washington, D.C.

Reading Adviser: Dr. Linda D. Labbo, Department of Reading Education,
College of Education, The University of Georgia

Let's See Library
Compass Point Books
Minneapolis, Minnesota

G. Small

Compass Point Books
3109 West 50th Street, #115
Minneapolis, MN 55410

Visit Compass Point Books on the Internet at *www.compasspointbooks.com* or e-mail your
request to *custserv@compasspointbooks.com*

On the cover: The Washington Monument

Photographs ©: Digital Stock, cover, 20; White House Collection, courtesy White House Historical
Association, 4; Photo Network/Jeff Greenberg, 6; Index Stock Imagery/Bill Bachmann, 8; Hulton/Archive by
Getty Images, 10; Bettmann/Corbis, 12; Stock Montage, 14; Getty Images/AFP Photo/Shawn Thew, 16; Getty
Images/AFP Photo/Tim Sloan, 18.

Editor: Catherine Neitge
Photo Researcher: Marcie C. Spence
Designers/Page Production: Melissa Kes and Jaime Martens/Les Tranby

Library of Congress Cataloging-in-Publication Data
Nobleman, Marc Tyler.
    The Washington Monument / by Marc Tyler Nobleman.
        p. cm. — (Let's see)
Includes bibliographical references and index.
Contents: What is the Washington Monument?—Where is the Washington Monument?—How big is the
Washington Monument?—Who made the Washington Monument?—When was the Washington Monument
built?—What problems occurred during the Washington Monument construction?—How has the Washington
Monument changed?—How can you see the Washington Monument?—What does the Washington Monument
mean to people?
ISBN 0-7565-0621-2
1. Washington Monument (Washington, D.C.)—Juvenile literature. 2. Washington, George, 1732-1799—
Monuments—Washington (D.C.)—Juvenile literature. 3. Washington (D.C.)—Buildings, structures, etc.—
Juvenile literature. [1. Washington Monument (Washington, D.C.) 2. National monuments.] I. Title. II. Series.
    F203.4.W3N73 2004
    975.3—dc22   2003014476

Table of Contents

NOTE: In this book, words that are defined in the glossary
are in **bold** the first time they appear in the text.

What Is the Washington Monument?

The Washington Monument is a structure that was built to honor George Washington. He was the first president of the United States. He is often called the Father of Our Country.

People admired and respected George Washington for many reasons. He was a brave soldier. He was a successful general in the American Revolution (1775–1783). He helped create the **Constitution**. He served two terms as president, from 1789 to 1797. After Washington died, Americans wanted to remember their beloved leader. They decided to build a memorial to Washington in the country's capital city, which is named after him.

◄ *George Washington is often called the Father of Our Country.*

Where Is the Washington Monument?

The Washington Monument is located on the National Mall in Washington, D.C. The Mall is a park that is 2 miles (3 kilometers) long. It connects the U.S. Capitol, which is the building where the U.S. Congress meets, with the Lincoln Memorial and the Washington Monument. A shorter part of the Mall connects the White House with the Jefferson Memorial. The Mall includes large areas of grass, fountains, pools, museums, and other memorials. It represents the heart of the capital city.

◀ *The Washington Monument is on the Mall near the Lincoln Memorial.*

8

How Big Is the Washington Monument?

The Washington Monument is a tall stone **obelisk.** This hollow shaft is one of the tallest freestanding **masonry** structures in the world. It is wider at the bottom than at the top. The top is shaped like a **pyramid.** The monument stands 555 feet 5 inches (169.29 meters) high. The observation level is 500 feet (152 m) high. That is 50 stories off the ground!

The width at the base is 55 feet (16 m) on each side. There are 36,491 stone blocks in the structure. The monument weighs 90,854 tons (82,421 metric tons). The walls are 15 feet (4.5 m) thick at the base and 18 inches (46 centimeters) thick at the observation level.

◀ *The staircase to the top of the Washington Monument has 897 steps. Since the early 1970s, people have not been allowed to climb the stairs to the top of the monument.*

Who Made the Monument?

In 1833, a group of people formed the Washington National Monument Society. They hoped to raise enough money to build a large memorial. In 1836, they held a contest to choose a design. Architect Robert Mills won the contest.

Mills's design included an obelisk, statues, and columns. It looked good, but it was too expensive. The society decided to build only an obelisk. It would cost $1 million to build. Members of the society needed help. They asked the states, Native American nations, and even foreign countries to send special stones of a certain type and size. These groups sent a total of 193 commemorative stones.

◄ *Robert Mills's design included a flat-topped obelisk, columns, a statue of George Washington in a chariot, and other statues.*

When Was the Washington Monument Built?

Construction of the Washington Monument began on July 4, 1848. That night, people celebrated and watched fireworks. About 20,000 people attended, including President James K. Polk.

Workers stopped building the monument in 1854, but it was not yet completed. Construction started again in 1880. The monument was finished in 1884.

The **dedication** ceremony was on February 21, 1885, the day before the 153rd anniversary of Washington's birth. Again, people celebrated and watched fireworks. The Washington Monument was officially opened on October 9, 1888.

◄ *The capstone was placed at the top on December 6, 1884. It was crowned with a 9-inch (23-centimeter) tip made of aluminum, which at that time was considered a precious metal.*

Why Did Construction Stop?

Many problems interrupted the construction of the Washington Monument. It stood only 152 feet (46 m) high when construction stopped in 1854. This was less than one-third of its planned height.

Political fights, bad leadership, a lack of money, and the Civil War (1861–1865) caused a long delay.

The problems started when thieves from a political party called the Know-Nothings stole one of the commemorative stones. This made people very upset, and they quit giving money for the monument. Then the Know-Nothings took over the project and did a terrible job. All of the problems were finally solved, and work resumed in 1880.

◄ *This photo taken in 1860 by famous photographer Mathew Brady shows how the Washington Monument stood unfinished for more than 25 years.*

How Can You See the Washington Monument?

Almost a million people visit the Washington Monument every year. People gather on the grounds for special occasions such as the Fourth of July. They have picnics and watch fireworks. From the Washington Monument, people can walk to the other memorials and monuments on the Mall.

The Washington Monument is open daily from 9 a.m. to 4:45 p.m., except Christmas. In the summer, it is open later. Tickets are required to enter the monument, but they are free. (There is a small charge for reserved tickets.) You can enjoy the monument from the outside any time you want. It is lit up at night.

◀ *Huge crowds of people gather near the Washington Monument to watch fireworks explode on the Fourth of July.*

How Do You Reach the Top?

For many years after the monument opened, people could climb to the top to enjoy the view. The monument also had an elevator powered by steam. It was used to complete the monument and then to carry passengers. It took 10 to 12 minutes to reach the top.

The first electrical elevator was installed in 1901. It held 35 passengers and took five minutes to reach the top. In 1959, a new elevator was installed that reached the top in 70 seconds. In 1998, a faster control panel allowed passengers to reach the top in 60 seconds.

In 2001, a new elevator cab with glass doors was installed. It allows visitors to view the commemorative stones in the stairwell as they go up.

◄ *The Washington Monument was shrouded in scaffolding and fabric when it was renovated and cleaned in the late 1990s.*

What Does the Monument Mean to People?

The Washington Monument is a tribute to George Washington. He led the American colonists in their fight to win independence from Great Britain. He helped form the new government and served as the first president of the United States.

The Washington Monument is a symbol of Washington's strength. It stands tall and straight, like he did. Washington was brave in war. He wanted the best for the people of the United States. He believed that Americans would have a bright future.

When people visit the Washington Monument, they remember what Washington did for his country.

◀ *The country's monument to George Washington stands straight and tall, a symbol of the first president's strength.*

Glossary

Constitution—the document stating the basic laws of the United States
dedication—an opening observance
masonry—something built of stone or brick by a worker called a mason

obelisk—a tall, four-sided shaft with a pointed top shaped like a pyramid
pyramid—a solid shape with triangular sides that meet at a point on top

Did You Know?

•   At the time it was completed, the Washington Monument was the world's tallest structure. It is still the tallest structure in Washington, D.C.

•   Through the years, changes have been made to the monument. In 1929, lights were installed at the top so aircraft could see the monument at night. In 1937, a circle of flags was placed around the monument, one flag for each state. As more states joined the Union, more flags were added. In 1976, a ramp was installed so people in wheelchairs could enter the monument's elevator.

•   The Washington Monument is built from materials from different states: white marble from Maryland and Massachusetts for the outside and granite from Maine for the inside.

•   The outside of the Washington Monument is two shades of white. The marble above 152 feet (46 m) is a different color than the marble below. That is because of the long pause in construction. The same kind of marble was used, but it came from different quarries and did not match perfectly.

Want to Know More?

In the Library

January, Brendan. *The National Mall.*
   Danbury, Conn.: Children's Press, 2000.
Santella, Andrew. *George Washington.*
   Minneapolis: Compass Point Books, 2001.
Schaefer, Lola. *The Washington Monument.*
   Crystal Lake, Ill.: Heinemann Library, 2002.

On the Web

For more information on the *Washington Monument,* use FactHound to track down Web sites related to this book.

1. Go to *www.compasspointbooks. com/facthound*
2. Type in this book ID: 0756506212
3. Click on the *Fetch It* button.

Your trusty FactHound will fetch the best Web sites for you!

Through the Mail

Washington Monument
900 Ohio Drive S.W.
Washington, DC 20024
To write for information about the Washington Monument

On the Road

Washington Monument
15th Street S.W.
Washington, DC
Metro stop: Smithsonian
202/426-6841
To visit the Washington Monument, which is open daily except Christmas.

Index

About the Author

Marc Tyler Nobleman has written more than 30 books for young readers. He has also written for a History Channel show called "The Great American History Quiz" and for several children's magazines including Nickelodeon, Highlights for Children, and Read (a Weekly Reader publication). He is also a cartoonist, and his single panels have appeared in more than 100 magazines internationally. He lives in Connecticut.